"This is the beginning of a new day. You have been given this day to use as you will.

You can waste it or use it for good.

What you do today is important because you are exchanging a day of your life for it.

When tomorrow comes, this day will be gone forever; in its place is something that you have left behind...let it be something good." ~ Unknown

Contents

Starting a Gift Basket Home Business

Have ever given any thought to the *huge* potential of a Gift Basket Home Business?

Even in today's uncertain economic climate there are people and businesses looking for a beautiful and original gift to give to friends, family, clients and employees. A well thought out and well-made Gift Basket could just be the answer.

…and who better to supply them than you?

This is the ideal small business for a Work at Home Mom (or Dad…). The opportunities for selling Gift Baskets are all around you, you just have to use a bit of imagination to find them.

That is what I have tried to cover in this book; the business opportunities and where to find them.

There are many markets for Gift Baskets and we will discuss some of these later on in this book.

Just a few to get your creative juices flowing are; home decorators, large corporations, small businesses and individuals – they are all potential clients for your Gift Basket home business enterprise.

You already know there is a demand for these Gift Baskets, so how will you cash in on that demand?

Well, first you need to understand your market; you need to find out who your customers will be and who they will be giving the Gift Basket to.

As with any new business you need to have a business plan.

Here are some topics to think about when preparing your Gift Basket home business plan:

1. Who are your customers?

2. What is your product range?

3. Who is your competition?

4. What will your USP (unique selling point) be? i.e. what will you offer that is different from your competition?

5. How will you finance your Gift Baskets home business?

6. How will you price your Gift Baskets?

7. How will you advertise?

Your first step is to get a large sheet of paper and write down the answers to the 7 questions above.

Write as many answers to each question as you can come up with. If you have someone you can 'brainstorm' with, it will really help you think up some original ideas.

This book will help you with some good ideas to help you with your business plan.

Once you have a few good answers to each question, it's time to put your business plan together.

Now print it out and stick it above your desk where you can see it each day.

This will serve to remind you the direction you want to go.

Your Customers

Two possible local customer bases are: individuals and local businesses.

In the beginning your customers will need a way to find out about your Gift Basket business.

So you will have to be creative about letting the world know about your new venture.

Gift Baskets fall into the category of crafts and they will do well being sold at craft fairs especially during the winter holiday selling season.

There are many other ways to sell your creations like distributing business cards (which you can get for free at www.vistaprint.com) or you could design and print some brochures to pass around or mail.

You could hand out flyers at functions and put up some posters in your local stores, your church notice board and anywhere else you can think of.

You could even advertise in your local free ad newspaper, online on craigslist, usfreeads etc.

Join the local chamber of Commerce and attend their networking meetings. Be sure to have a stock of your business cards to hand out.

These meetings are invaluable for making business contacts.

An Internet Presence

You can widen your customer base by selling online through a website.

You could join a gift selling company that provides the products and website as an affiliate or you can create your own Gift Baskets and either design your own website or have one built for you by a professional.

Be careful to research your chosen web designer as the cost can be prohibitive if you are not careful and the results are not always what you expected.

Your website can advertise your Gift Basket business by offering informative articles to the new mom, the newly engaged bride-to-be or the business owner who is looking for ideas for rewarding his top sales people etc.

You can put photographs of a couple of your most popular Gift Baskets on your website to give a potential customer an idea of what to expect when they order a Gift Basket from you.

As you get more and more business you should always take a photograph of every Gift Basket you make and put it on a 'gallery' page on your website.

Make sure you ask your customers for a written testimonial when you deliver a Gift Basket.

Update your website regularly to keep potential clients informed of new ideas, new baskets etc.

Another lucrative outlet for your gift baskets is Amazon. It is really easy to sell using Amazon's platform and you won't have to look for customers – Amazon have millions…

Go to Amazon.com and scroll to the bottom of the page.

Click on 'Sell on Amazon' as shown.

Follow the simple instructions to set up your Amazon Sellers Account.

Start off with the 'Individual Sellers' account, then when you are selling a lot and it becomes cost effective, you can move up to the 'Professional Sellers' account.

You will have to think carefully about the type of gift baskets you offer for sale through Amazon because you will have to send your products by mail and not all baskets will be suitable for delivery this way.

Gist baskets containing non-perishable goods such as Spa Baskets, Baby Baskets etc. are good for posting providing you choose the actual basket carefully.

For instance, a Baby Gift Basket could be created in a beautiful holdall that the recipient will be able to use for carrying all baby's equipment around.

When you are speaking to a client, you could offer a gift or discount if they can give you some recommendations.

For everyone who orders a product through a recommendation you would send the recommender a gift or a 30% discount off their next gift basket order. This works especially well with corporate clients as they do a lot of networking.

So, now you know that you can sell Gift Baskets using the craft show circuit, traditional word of mouth and business marketing tools like business cards, flyers, and brochures, as well as online tools like a blog or a website and probably the best of the online methods, Amazon.

Types of Gift Baskets

What Gift Basket categories will you offer?

Some of the more popular suggestions are:

- Baby Shower

- Bath and Body (Spa)

- Customized Baskets

- Father's Day

- Gourmet Food

- Mother's Day

- Romantic Date/Get away

- Wedding Shower

- Moving House

- Christmas Basket

- Just Because…

- And so many more…

What about visiting the car dealers in your area?

I know that, in my area, they used to put a bouquet of flowers in the back seat of every car they sold.

Not anymore – they put one of my Gift Baskets in each car now.

Coming up to Christmas a lot of employers like to give their employees a gift. I have a lot of corporate customers who buy Gift Baskets and then staple a bonus voucher to the basket as a 'Thank You' to each of their employees.

Send a leaflet around to the local business owners in your area suggesting your Gift Baskets as their Holiday gift to their staff.

At this time a lot of stores run raffles or competitions, offer to make them some beautiful Gift Baskets as prizes.

Do something different like, health foods, chocolate or even a luxury gourmet basket.

Around November time produce a leaflet introducing your 'prize' Gift Baskets to stores around your locality. In the leaflet explain that you will tailor the baskets to the store.

For instance, for a pet shop you will create a prize basket for dogs, cats, birds etc., for a craft shop you will create a basket of craft supplies and so on.

Another excellent idea to get your business known is to donate one or two baskets to the neighborhood organization that greets new residents with goodies from local businesses.

If there is no such organization in your neighborhood then you could start one yourself.

If you are starting this service yourself, you could visit the local stores and ask for a donation to include in the basket and agree to include their business details in the Gift Baskets in return.

You would provide a welcome gift to the purchasers of a new home with a Gift basket containing some of the essential items they will need and perhaps won't find until they unpack their mountain of boxes from the move.

You could include items such as coffee and biscuits, a pair of mugs and a spoon, a small pair of scissors, some soft slippers, some soap and a hand towel etc.

These baskets could also include a notebook, a calendar and coupons from local businesses to entice the new resident to sample their wares.

If your basket is made up of donations from local businesces, put a leaflet in the bottom of the basket thanking each contributor along with their contact details.

Don't forget to include your business details. You could add a label to these baskets that say something like, "A Warm Welcome to Our Neighborhood. (Basket supplied by [Your business name])". Clip your business card to the side of the basket where it will be seen by the recipient.

Contact the realtor and suggest this service when you notice that a property is for sale.

An on-going contract could be agreed that will benefit both the realtor and you.

Stock

Decide how you will handle stock and how you will market your Gift Baskets home business.

Will you make up a stock or make your Gift Baskets to order? Obviously if you intend to sell at Craft Fairs you will have to make up a stock of your Gift Baskets

Will you sell to local customers only or will you have a website to market to a wider customer base?

As in any business, being able to bounce ideas off others who are in business is good and can help you to avoid some of the more common and costly mistakes.

You will be wise to network with local businesses in your area to help spread the word about your new Gift Basket business and to gain goodwill in your community which will help with obtaining suppliers and customers.

Maybe you could join your local council group – networking with other businesses is a great way to get more business yourself. Ask other local businesses which are the best organizations to join for networking purposes.

Try and source as much of your Gift Basket contents locally if you can. This is very good for creating a feeling of goodwill with your suppliers who may well think of you when they want to give a gift.

Paying attention to the needs of your customers, satisfying those needs, planning your business right from the start and networking are all ways to assure you will be a success in the Gift Basket business arena.

Who would want a Gift Basket?

You have an outlet to meet a need for a wide variety of gift giving occasions. A Gift Basket can be created for a mom-to-be, a bride-to-be, or a recently retired teacher.

Here are a few more occasions that could warrant a Gift Basket purchase.

Someone needs to attend a baby shower; someone else wants to give a memorable baby's first birthday gift.

A mom deserves a beautiful reminder of how loved she is or your best friend needs a 'welcome to the neighborhood' basket of goodies.

An employee wants to reward an employee for reaching targets.

A child needs a 'Get Well' gift to help entertain him when he is unwell.

Any of these events are reasons for creating a Gift Basket. The baskets can be sturdy, reusable, and can hold many items.

A Gift Basket is not just one, but many reasons for the giver to be remembered for their thoughtfulness.

Creating a Gift Basket not only answers a need, but also allows the giver a chance to use their imagination to create a lasting impression on the recipient.

Creating a Gift Basket can be a very satisfying task.

There are many websites that will illustrate how to create your masterpiece – this book is aimed more at the business side with great unique ideas for your new business.

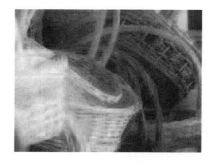

There are lots of places to buy original containers

Where to Start

Consulting with your Client

- Meet with your client or send them a questionnaire to find out a bit about the purpose of the Gift Basket.

- Find out about the person who is to receive the Gift Basket. If you are creating a basket for a client, get them to write down a bit about the recipient.

- Together you and your client should choose a theme for your basket.

- Decide with the client if the items in the basket will be functional, fun, romantic, or personal.

- Focus on the needs of the person you are creating the Gift Basket for.

- Presentation is everything. Appeal to the eye, the sense of smell and the emotions.

- Leave your personal mark on the Gift Basket, like a business card in the bottom of the basket.

- Choose a basket or container style that fits the occasion (color, size, material).

You need to be clear about your charges; you do not want to spend time creating a beautiful basket only to find it is more expensive than your client had anticipated. For this reason I always take payment before I create the basket; or at least 50% non-refundable deposit.

Supplies

You will need some basic supplies for creating a Gift Basket and they are:

- The basket or container

- Items to put in the basket

- Gift wrapping paper

- Shredded paper filling

- Ribbon

- Cellophane, tulle or other see through gift wrap.

- Any other adornments that you think would add to the look of the basket.

For some online suppliers of Gift Basket constructing items check out the companies on the last page of this book.

At the time of writing, these contacts were available but, if they are not, simply do a Google search for gift basket material suppliers.

Putting it all together

Now comes the fun part - putting it all together.

Wrap each of the items in gift wrap that fits the gift giving event.

Shred some paper to use as filling or use the ready shredded paper that you bought (sold in craft stores) and put on the bottom of the basket.

Place the wrapped gifts so that they are arranged nicely (some vertical, some horizontal).

Push the shredded paper in between the gifts.

Remember to include your business card.

Put the filled basket on the middle of a sheet of cellophane gift wrap (clear or colored).

Make sure you have a piece big enough to cover the entire basket. You may need two sheets if you have a large basket.

Bring all the sides of the cellophane up over the basket and tie with a long colorful ribbon.

Tack your special greeting card onto the cellophane at the top or attach to the ends of the ribbon.

In the next few pages we're going to look at some of the types of Gift Baskets you can create and sell.

Check out YouTube for ideas and instructions on the construction of your Gift Baskets.

Gift Basket Instructions - How to Make a Beautiful Gift Basket - Giftbasketappeal

http://youtu.be/0F3ceV-bQrs

Here is one video I found that gives very detailed instructions but there are loads more, just put 'Making Gift Baskets' in the search bar of YouTube.

But be aware; you can spend a lot of time watching these instead of making a start with your first creation.

Gift Basket Ideas

Baby Gift Baskets

It is really great fun to create and sell Baby Gift Baskets.

Everyone loves babies and finding small gifts to give on any baby occasion such as Baby Showers, Baby's First Birthday, or a New Baby Welcome Basket is a fun part of your job.

Sometimes the occasion will have a theme to it, like with a Baby Shower and sometimes you will know the sex of the child and can design the Baby Gift Basket around a boy or girl theme.

You can get really creative with a Baby Gift Basket.

The basket itself can be a useful item.

It can be a place to hold diaper supplies, or it can be a gift in itself, like a stroller (in place of the basket) that you fill with beautifully wrapped gifts (the seats and the stroller basket).

You can use a baby bathtub and fill it with bath time supplies.

Baby Gift Basket Ideas

There are many gifts you could choose from to fill the basket including:

Diapers, bath items, diaper care items, outfits, homecoming blankets, bibs, feeding needs, and soothing needs like pacifiers and lullaby music.

You can also fill the Baby Gift Basket with items for the mom like nursing items, pampering Gift certificates to have her nails painted or to a spa, soft slippers or a coupon for free babysitting service.

Other Gift ideas are:

Changing pads for the changing table, baby quilts, a diaper stacker, crib mobiles, a baby memory book, socks and sleepers, rattles and other soft toys, and also nursery decorations that will appeal to the sight or sound needs of the new baby.

There are everyday needs that can be turned into gifts like spoons, baby wipes, ointments, lotions, washcloths and hooded towels, baby cloth books, bath toys, and a diaper bag.

Don't forget plenty of receiving blankets, and lots of either cloth or disposable diapers depending on mom's preference.

Themed Baby Gift Baskets are really fun to make up and require that you ask what the theme will be in advance.

Let the organizer of the event know that you will be using the theme in your gift selection (just in case they think about changing the theme).

The theme can be used not only in selecting the gifts to place in the basket, but in choosing the basket as well.

Baskets can come in all sizes, shapes and colors. Keeping the theme in mind when selecting your basket and gifts will result in a more satisfying finished product.

When making a Baby Gift Basket for a baby shower or new baby, make sure you check with the gift registries for ideas.

Obviously budget will play a big part in the gifts that are used to create the Gift Basket, so make sure that your client knows what s/he will be getting for the price that they pay.

You don't want them to think that they will be getting a Baby Bathtub filled to the brim with luxury items if they only have a budget of $25!

Always be absolutely clear about what the client can expect to receive for their budget.

Food Gift Baskets

Holidays and Food Gift Baskets just go together.

They are a favorite holiday gift to receive and to give.

Food Gift Baskets are crowd pleasers at family functions and corporate events.

They brighten up a party and turn any party into a real celebration.

Supplies are plentiful and can be obtained locally. You really do not have to sell the customer on the appeal of food for any of their gift giving needs.

Baskets can be useful after the contents are enjoyed.

So a Food Gift Basket is the gift that keeps on giving, even after the last morsel of food has been devoured, especially if the basket is durable.

Food Basket Ideas

Food Gift Baskets can contain any variety of food, beverages, desserts, fruit, candy, even fresh food.

To give great value to your customer, make sure that your creations contain more food than filler, are packed neatly and securely so they arrive intact and in perfect condition.

All basket creations, especially food ones, should have the option to customize them at no additional charge. It is a wise business decision to give more value to the customer than they are expecting.

This will keep them coming back.

When making deliveries of Food Gift Baskets it is wise to avoid contents that may spoil or melt in warm weather. Cold packs could be used that are designed for the purpose or the food selection can be modified for warm weather.

When designing a Food Gift Basket around a theme or hobby it may be necessary, even beneficial, to include non-food items but sparingly.

Examples would be: pacifiers, diapers, stuffed toys for a baby shower Food Gift Basket along with food items or breath mints, music CD, flowers for a romantic Food Gift Basket.

Let your theme or hobby selection be your guide for what would be an appropriate item to be included.

It would also be prudent to know how well the customer knows the intended recipient and what the gift giving occasion is.

Customized Food Gift Baskets can be fun to design and prepare. Use filler wisely and position the non-food items so that the food takes center stage and the non-food items are simply used to add more interest to the basket.

There should always be more food product than filler in the basket and don't forget ribbons, bows and cellophane.

Another Food Gift Basket pleaser is to include one or more of the following: a candle, small non-food gift, wine glasses when wine is included, and personal grooming products when appropriate.

Gourmet Gift Baskets

When an item is described as being "gourmet" it is because it represents an item chosen by a person who has discriminating taste in food or wine and anticipates great enjoyment when the item is consumed or used.

Some associate the word with excessive refinement or luxury to the extreme. It conjures up pictures of pure enjoyment and immense satisfaction.

To be a Gourmet Gift Basket it must contain items of the highest quality that have been perfectly prepared and presented with a great sense of style and artistic flair.

The Gift Baskets home business customer sometimes overlooks Gourmet Gift Baskets.

It could be helpful to steer your customer towards the Gourmet Gift Basket when they are trying to decide on an original theme or gift.

Gourmet Basket Ideas

Some ideas you could suggest are baskets with the following combinations:

- Assorted Chocolates and Fruits

- Gourmet Coffees and Nuts

- Gourmet Food and Wine

- Smoked Salmon and Caviar

- Fine Oils and Vinegars (if the recipient is an aspiring chef)

Food and beverages are not the only ingredients that can be placed in a Gourmet Gift Basket.

You can suggest to your customer that you include a good book, small personal items, cooking utensils for the chef or flowers.

Luxury cookies and candles are also good additions.

If you are making a Get Well Gourmet Gift Basket you may suggest that they order some comfort foods such as cheeses, crackers, meat and nuts.

These also make great office party baskets or family event baskets.

The receiver and the giver appreciate the Gourmet Gift Basket for its uniqueness and for the wonderful items contained in them.

There are several types of Gourmet Gift Baskets, and any one of them will sure to please the discerning customer.

Such as:

- The Gourmet Coffee Gift Basket - filled with an assortment of gourmet coffees or coffee bean roasts, and usually a mix of nuts, fruit or cookies/biscuits.

- Gourmet Cookie Basket, cookies come in bars, brownies and cakes that can be arranged in beautiful tins, towers, boxes or special Baskets.

- Gourmet Cheese and/or Wine – you could include a pair of crystal wine glasses.

- Gourmet Meats – obviously this type of basket cannot be prepared in advance.

You can also include non-food items to complete any theme or occasion.

Whatever your customer chooses to include in the gourmet Gift Basket, you can be sure that their expectations will be for high quality, extreme good taste and superb value.

It is your responsibility as the Gift Baskets provider to provide for these gourmet expectations and ensure that both the giver and the recipient is not disappointed.

Excellent customer service is a necessity if you want your clients to return for more gift baskets.

Unique Gift Baskets

One of the great things about running a Gift Basket business is that you can use your creativity to design some really unique Gift Baskets for your personal and corporate clients.

Many of these are themed baskets that are special and require some attention to detail.

Unique Gift Baskets Ideas

There are many occasions where business clients may request something unique such as:

- Conventions

- Bon Voyage

- Get Well

- Holiday

- Retirements

- Special Corporate Events

- Presentations (for Sales etc.)

- Get Well

These events may require a customized Gift Basket that demands quality, unique selection and attention to detail.

Your personal, individual customers will have many occasions where they may need unique Gift Baskets such as:

- Shower Baskets Baby Gift Baskets

- Mother's Day and Father's Day Gift Baskets

- Food, Gourmet or Fruit Baskets

- Men's Gifts or Women's Gifts

- Gifts for teens or for kids especially birthdays

- Housewarming Gift Baskets

- Sport team Gifts for that big game,

- Sympathy Gift Baskets

- Wedding

- Anniversary.

The Container

Unique Gift Baskets are just one way for your clients to send a gift that will be personalized and give a lasting impression to commemorate a very special event, day or memory.

The container you use will serve as a reminder of the occasion.

You can make your Gift Baskets home business unique not only by the style of your baskets and what goes in them, but by using a unique shape of basket.

For instance, you could use a beautiful wicker picnic basket for a woman or a wicker fishing basket for a man, to make the gift unique.

You can also set your Gift Baskets home business above your competitors by offering a local delivery service, more payment options, or a complimentary service like perhaps a stationary service where you would handle party invitations.

What makes your home business unique will set you apart from not only other gift giving businesses, but also the local businesses in general.

As well as the exceptional quality of your Gift Baskets, this could be your friendly customer service, your prompt personal phone response, or your low prices for quality gifts.

What goes into your baskets can be unique in how they are wrapped, or in the style of presentation, the lining of the basket, the basket itself or in how it is delivered to the customer.

You can make your creations unique by adding an unexpected bonus to every basket ordered. It will be appreciated and should complement the basket selected by your customer.

It is up to you to come up with a USP (unique selling point) for your Gift Basket business to make it stand out from all the rest.

Holiday Gift Baskets

Every year personal and corporate customers struggle to think of gifts to give to clients and family members that will fit budgets and please at the same time.

Social protocol for most businesses is to network with other business associates and exchange gifts at holiday times.

One gift of value and practicality is the Holiday Gift Basket.

As a Gift Baskets home business owner you can provide customers with a wide selection of Holiday Gift Baskets that feature food, candy, cookies, wine, gourmet selections, non-food items and personalized gifts.

There are many holidays throughout the year that lend themselves to the opportunity to give gifts.

Holiday Gift Baskets Ideas

- Christmas

- Easter

- Father's Day

- Mother's Day

- Valentine's Day

- Standard Holiday Gift Baskets

- Children's Holiday Gift Baskets

- Thanksgiving Holiday Gift Baskets

- Halloween Holiday Gift Baskets

Holiday Gift Baskets lend themselves to several great themes that include: baby, chocolate, coffee, cookie, kids, men, women, those who garden, those who play golf; those who love gourmet foods, the graduate, those who celebrate good health, patriotic holidays, romantic, spa baskets and many, many more.

There is a wide assortment of food items that can be placed in Holiday Gift Baskets including: meats, cheeses, hard candies, soft candies, gourmet coffees, Belgian chocolates, cheesecakes, cookies, and snack items.

Corporate Holiday Gift Baskets

Corporate Gift Baskets for holiday giving offer many different themes from fruit to chocolate, to the executive Wine Baskets.

Corporate Baskets can be quite elaborate with a high price tag or they can be reasonably priced.

Corporate Holiday Baskets are given to employees in appreciation, to business clients to thank them for their business or their partnership and to special employees for outstanding achievement and also executives for the dedication they provide the firms.

Corporate Holiday Gift Baskets may contain personalized items as well as snacks, candy, coffee and teas, wine, crackers, snacks, cookies, gourmet foods, and personalized gifts.

Personal Holiday Gift Baskets

Personalized individual Holiday Gift Baskets are perfect for that hard to buy for relative, the holiday gift exchange or the family gift to someone special.

A Christmas Gift Basket can be filled with all sorts of festive items; you could even include a CD of Christmas songs.

A Holiday Gift Basket is the perfect way to show your appreciation for anyone during the holidays and can contain many wonderful selections including: continental gourmet foods, an all occasion picnic basket when food makes a statement and commands center stage.

Customized Holiday Gifts are perfect for those holidays or special occasions when you want to send your very best wishes for baby, birthdays, for sending sympathy, get well wishes, for wedding celebrations or as a housewarming celebration.

Spa Gift Baskets

One really terrific offering for your customers is a Spa Gift Basket. What better way for your customers to show they care for someone than to give them a Spa Gift Basket.

Spa Gift Baskets are great for an engagement, vacations, the workaholic, as a special thank you or as a Mother's Day Gift.

As a Gift Baskets home business it is important to keep the cost down for your customer whilst still providing a quality product. Spa Gift Baskets can be an economical gift option for your clients.

Spa Gift Baskets Ideas

Popular items include scented candles and bath salts, bath fizzies, bath oil, bath sponge or brush.

Don't forget to pamper the feet by providing foot products like scrubs for heels and foot lotions.

Body sprays are another good addition.

To keep the same scent as the bath products in the Spa Gift Baskets, make sure that you use products from the same range.

A Spa Gift Basket can be really relaxing when it contains loofahs, glycerin soaps, bath oils, scented candles, and body lotions.

Don't forget items for after the bath/spa like a favorite hot beverage (tea or coffee) in a tantalizing flavor just perfect for soothing nerves and calming after a long day.

Include items that will indulge the senses and calm a busy mind.

A pumice stone, foot lotion and a nail brush for the feet. To massage away tense muscles a wooden massager is a perfect additional gift.

The gifts could even be arranged in a colorful straw hat, purse or beach bag to add originality to the Spa Gift Basket.

The Gift Basket home business owner succeeds by meeting the needs of the customer and thinking ahead to anticipate additional needs.

Adding to a Spa Gift Basket with accessories will extend the enjoyment.

Adding value to the Gift Basket is one way to ensure that your customer remembers you and tells their friends about the great service that you offer.

The Spa Gift Basket can contain more personal gift items than would be appropriate for most corporate gift giving.

Spa Gift Baskets do make wonderful Mother's Day gifts, a gift for a new bride, or a valentine gift.

As an added surprise you might include a pedicure gift certificate.

Decorate the Spa Gift Basket in soft pastel colors with flowing ribbons and a Gift card with a chocolate mint tucked in the envelope for a nice touch.

Doing the little extras for your customer will add value.

Value and customer service is what gives you the kind of reputation that gets talked about and your name will be passed around.

Word of mouth is free advertising and is worth its weight in gold.

Custom Gift Baskets

Custom Gift Baskets are those that your customer designs so that it is special and unique for their individual needs.

They make the choices and you make the Gift Basket.

You will obviously have to help guide them towards gifts that are suitable for the occasion but it is great fun to collaborate with clients to design a fabulous Custom Gift Basket.

Custom Gift Baskets Ideas

Custom Gift Baskets vary in content but may contain gourmet food items, pre-packaged items like specialist pastas, candy, coffee or hot chocolate envelopes, cheeses or fruit, chocolates (except in warm weather), flowers, wine or beer, clothing, custom or personalized items, certificates, sporting accessories, toys or personal care items.

When offering a Custom Gift Basket creation you would have to be able to show customers examples of what their basket could include so they have something to choose from.

One way to showcase custom selections would be to have a portfolio of creations that you have made previously to show the prospective client.

It would be great if you have a couple of testimonials from satisfied clients.

Another idea would be to make up example baskets from your own ideas and then photograph them.

You could also type up a list of possible gift items to include. You would create this list using local suppliers so that you could be assured of having the items when ordered.

Custom Gift Baskets are created with the recipient in mind so that each item in it is personalized to the needs or taste of the intended receiver.

These choices can involve color scheme, shape, size and color of the basket even the make-up of the basket.

The basket might not even be a basket, but a container or large item like a baby stroller for a baby shower or ice bucket for a Wedding Gift Basket.

Wedding or Romantic Gift Baskets can be covered in Tulle, which is a sheer netting, to add to the pleasing effect. You could add romantic CD's to these baskets.

Custom Gift Baskets are as unique as the person or event being celebrated.

Custom Gift Baskets are also unique in price structure as they cannot be priced ahead of time, but are priced according to the items included and based on the basket itself.

Any time there is a product that is customized, the customer and the receiver of the Gift Basket will feel special.

Remember that your client may need assistance when putting together the Custom Gift Basket creation so be ready with some inventive and original suggestions.

Wine Gift Baskets

With a Wine Gift Basket you have two potential markets, the wine business owner and the wine lover.

The wine business owner could utilize your service to provide a unique way to present new lines to potential customers. They could also use Gift Baskets to give their customers a holiday gift.

Wine is elegant and perfect for intimate gifts, corporate gifts and celebratory gift giving.

Gift Baskets are a creative and thoughtful way to show you care about the special event or person receiving the Gift Basket.

Your clients will enjoy a good selection of wines and complimentary gift items or foods.

Combining the wines with the idea of a Gift Basket gives you the business edge because you can cover all the wine giving occasions, whilst covering a broad range of potential clients.

Wine Gift Baskets Ideas

Here are some potential clients and events for Wine Gift Baskets:

- A Wine Business owner who wants an original way to showcase new products.

- A couple celebrating their wedding anniversary - the basket may contain an assortment of wines that were available the year they were married

- Someone who is beginning a wine career

- Corporate Anniversaries or celebrations of achievement

- Honeymoon (Champagne, glasses and chocolates)

- Vacation

- Retirement

- Business Relocation

- Military achievement or advancement

Wine Gift Baskets come in different shapes, sizes and price ranges. Obviously, the more vintage the wine, the more expensive the basket price tag will be.

Wine selection is varied and can be tailored to the occasion being celebrated or the type of basket being prepared (gourmet food for example).

A Wine Gift Basket may also be themed around a particular country and the wine selections could be those that are popular in that country (California, U.S.A or from France, Italy, or Spain).

Including a pair of quality glasses in a Wine Gift Basket is another nice touch.

Car Dealer Gift Baskets

Speak to all the car dealers in your area about giving a Gift Basket with each car they sell instead of the usual bunch of flowers.

Impress on them the uniqueness of a Gift Basket.

Everyone will remember the car dealer that went the extra mile to give a thoughtful gift to their valued customer.

You can discuss with each dealer what they would like to put into the Gift Basket.

You could put in a bottle of wine with a couple of nice glasses along with some cheese and crackers.

Or what about some car themed gifts such as car air fresheners, de-icer, silver key ring, torch or even some car seat covers.

Dog Lovers Gift Basket

There are lots of people who absolutely adore their dog.

What about making a few Dog Lovers Gift Baskets?

You could include things like a squeaky toy, a rubber ball, a photo frame, a dog brush, rawhide bones, a collar charm, packs of dog treats and a luxury dog blanket.

If the giver is a good friend of the recipient, you could include some personalized items such as a keyring with the dogs photo in or a beautiful framed photo.

Get Well Gift Baskets

A Get Well Gift Basket is an excellent gift for someone who is feeling 'under the weather' It is a great and thoughtful alternative to the traditional bunch of flowers.

When you create a Get Well Gift Basket for a client you should find out a little about the proposed recipient so that you can make the Gift Basket more personal.

These types of baskets are great for children - you can include all sorts of small surprises for them to unwrap. You could include a stuffed toy and a hairbrush set for girls or a toy car and coloring book and crayons for boys.

A delivery service is usually appreciated as the giver doesn't need to be visiting to make sure that the recipient receives a thoughtful gift from them.

Even your corporate clients may appreciate the Get Well Gift Basket service. If a client, employee or just an acquaintance is unwell, what better way to show that the company is thinking about them?

Sometimes a company may want to donate something to a hospital as a good-will gesture and what better way than to give a Gift Basket to each of the patients in the children's ward or a Gift Basket to each of the residents of a nursing home. Suggest this in your promotional literature – it can be a great PR product.

There are lots of situations where a Get Well Gift Basket could be an appropriate and appreciated gift.

Valentines Day Gift Basket

When love is in the air, lots of people are looking for that special gift for the love of their life.

A Valentine's Day Gift Basket could be the answer.

When it is coming up to Valentine's Day, make sure that you have plenty of supplies to help you to create that very special gift for your clients.

Be sure to order some tulle for wrapping, red ribbon for bows and decoration, lots of shredded paper in either red or white and, if you happen to see anything that is heart shaped make sure that you buy it for your Valentine's Day Gift Basket inventory.

Some ideas for the Valentines Day Gift Basket include luxury chocolates, good quality candy, a romantic CD, a custom written love poem (yet another service that you could offer), scented candles and of course beautiful fresh flowers.

You could use heart shaped baskets and, for a woman, you could add a little bit of costume jewelry to add a bit of sparkle.

For a man you could add some chocolate body paint or a nicely decorated promissory note from the giver.

You could even advertise the **'Valentine's Day Engagement Gift Basket'.**

A Valentines Day Engagement Basket may help some of the less imaginative men create a memorable and romantic proposal.

The engagement ring could be placed in the bottom of the gift basket underneath all the other little gifts or given pride of place in the centre of the basket.

Don't forget to include a bottle of Champagne and two quality glasses in the Engagement Gift Basket.

Gift Baskets for Men

It is often difficult to buy a gift for a man.

A Gift Basket could provide a thoughtful and practical solution.

You could be inventive when choosing the container or basket to hold the gifts.

For a keen gardener you could use a decorative watering can or bucket or even a pair of Wellington boots (obviously new ones…).

For the fishing enthusiast, you could use a wicker fishing basket.

For a sports enthusiast you could decorate the basket with their favorite team colors. Include a replica team shirt and lots of small gifts around the team such as key fobs, caps etc. You could even include a pair of tickets to an upcoming game.

Most men love candy so you could include some of his favorites.

A Car Care Gift Basket for the man who loves his car. You could include a large sponge, car wax, a brush for the tyres, a window cleaning pad or even a promissory note for washing the car etc.

Golf enthusiasts could have a Gift Basket containing different colored golf balls, tees, golf club covers, a golf hat and so on...

For the man who is not sports mad, a gift basket containing his favorite wine or beer along with some good cheeses and luxury cookies.

A personalized glass for his favorite tipple is a thoughtful addition.

As a Gift Basket Business Owner, you are the person who needs to have some original ideas for your gift baskets.

Your clients will be asking you what are the best items to include and it is up to you to provide some original and thoughtful suggestions.

Manicure Gift Basket

A Manicure Gift Basket is a great gift and can be fit into a smaller size basket whilst not compromising on quality content.

Things that you could include: Nail polish, nail polish remover, cotton balls, emery boards, nail buffer, cuticle cream, hand lotion and for that extra special touch, a voucher for a manicure at your local salon.

Book Lovers Gift Basket

If the client knows the recipient really well, together you could choose some great books, for a Book Lovers Gift Basket. Then you could include a luxury bookmark, a comfortable cushion, a book token, a desk lamp etc.

Naughty Gift Baskets

These are great sellers for the adult market.

If you don't mind buying the gifts to put into these you can include chocolate body paint, candles, some edible underwear – use your imagination for this…

Store Gift Baskets

This is a great idea coming up to holiday times.

Speak to local store owners and offer to make up gift baskets which include their products.

For example, a farm shop could include cured meat, free range eggs, cheeses, etc.

A pharmacy could include perfumes, bath products etc.

A toy shop could include lots of small toys and you could do a Boys Gift Basket and a Girls Gift Basket.

The stores could then sell these baskets at a premium price.

So, as you can see, the ideas for Gift Baskets are endless. I have given you a start and if you use your imagination, I'm sure that you could come up with a lot more.

By providing lots of helpful suggestions and Gift Basket options to your clients you will be helping your Gift Basket business to grow.

Satisfied clients always tell their friends and they will return to you when they need another interesting and original gift.

Promoting Your Gift Basket Business

The Gift Baskets home business is a thriving business when the smart entrepreneur learns how to target this very lucrative corporate market.

Sending out a letter including photos of your Holiday Gift Baskets with your company business card and website if available, several months in advance will give busy executives the time they need to outsource their Gift giving chores into your capable hands. Follow up with a phone call to ask if they have received your Gift ideas.

If you are marketing locally you may consider stopping by each business with a small sampler Basket and photographs of your other creations, for the business owner along with your business card of course.

Contact realtors, stores, car dealers, churches etc.

The only limit is your imagination.

Providing a Gift Basket Service will definitely make you a good and steady income IF you put in some effort and imagination.

Find a USP (unique selling point) and then devise some great marketing plans and you will be on your way.

My Final Words: There really are 100's of different opportunities for a Gift Basket home business but ultimately, it is up to you to make your business a profitable one.

This book is intended to help you to set up a Gift Basket Home Business. It does not guarantee any income whatsoever – that is in your own hands.

If you **'TAKE ACTION'** now, you could have a profitable business.

However, if you do nothing then you will earn nothing – your call…

This book is for the use of the purchaser, please do not attempt to copy the contents or distribute the book in any way.

Some Gift Baskets Supplies Vendors

Here are some online places you can purchase supplies with phone numbers where available:

http://www.GiftBasketsupplies.com/

888-224-7110 Fax 714-634-4424

http://www.macpaper.com/

800-486-5783 or 316-772-0311

http://www.bluebonnetvillage.com/basket1.htm

This website has a list of different suppliers and their contact details

http://www.americaBasket.com

1-800-262-9727

http://www.creativeGiftpackaging.com/

1-866-443-8706

http://www.traveltins.com – candles for your baskets

http://www.nsgaonline.com/

877-486-7884

Made in the USA
Lexington, KY
10 April 2014